THE ART OF WAR
Know Who You Are Fi

MW01106948

Self published by Create Space: David Delontae Brown
Mindavidbrown85@gmail.com

Book Design copyright: CreateSpace.com
Interior Design copyright: CreateSpace.com & David D. Brown

Published in the United States of America
ISBN: 978-1492752899
Study guide to Spiritual Warfare

INDEX

THE ART
OF
WAR

KNOW WHO YOU ARE FIGHTING...

ONE

THE ART OF WAR

GETTING IN THE FIGHT MODE; A TRAINING THAT MOLDS, CORRECTS, OR PERFECTS THE MENTAL FACULTIES OR MORAL CHARACTER, A MODE WHERE YOU'RE TIRED OF THE ENEMY.

In the Military there is discipline, and it is a practice from the Bible, We need discipline.
MATTHEW 11:12 *AND FROM THE DAYS OF JOHN THE BAPTIST UNTIL* <u>*NOW*</u> *THE KINGDOM OF HEAVEN SUFFERETH VIOLENCE AND THE VIOLENT TAKE IT BY* <u>*FORCE.*</u>

When is now?   RIGHT NOW
How does the Kingdom of God suffer?
VIOLENTLY
What is the Kingdom of God? GOD'S WAY OF DOING THINGS
Where is the Kingdom of God? WITHIN YOU
LUKE 17:20-21

When you begin doing things God's way things happen and therefore the enemy is mad and begins to attack when we make up our minds to live God's way. This is why we of the Kingdom must take it back <u>*BY FORCE.*</u>

Let's define violent; extreme force, sudden intense activity, almost like some one getting raped, it's by force not by choice. It's a violent attack on ones life.

2 CORINTHIANS 10:3 FOR THOUGH WE WALK IN THE FLESH, WE DO NOT WAR AFTER THE FLESH.

1 CORINTHIANS 10:13 THERE HATH NO TEMPTATIONTAKEN YOU BUT SUCH AS IS COMMON TO MAN: BUT GOD IS FAITHFUL, WHO WILL NOT SUFFER YOU TO BE TEMPTED ABOVE THAT YE ARE ABLE; BUT WILL WITH THE TEMPTATIONALSO MAKE A WAY TO ESCAPE, THAT YE MAY BE ABLE TO BEAR IT.

- *EVERY TEMPTATION IS A FLESH TEMPTAION*
- *BUT THE ESCAPE IS SPIRITUAL*

EPHESIANS 6:10-14 FINALLY, MY BRETHREN, BE STRONG IN THE LORD, AND IN THE POWER OF HIS MIGHT. PUT ON THE WHOLE ARMOUR OF GOD, THAT YE MAY BE ABLE TO STAND AGAINST THE WILES OF THE DEVIL, FOR WE WRESTLE NOT AGAINST FLESH AND BLOOD, BUT AGAINST PRINCIPALITIES, AGAINST POWERS, AGAINST THE RULERS OF THE DARKNESS OF THIS WORLD, AGAINST SPIRITUAL WICKEDNESS IN HIGH PLACES. WHEREFORE TAKE UNTO YOU THE WHOLE ARMOUR OF GOD THAT YE MAY BE ABLE TO WITH STAND IN THE EVIL DAY, AND HAVING DONE ALL TO STAND, STAND THEREFORE.....

3 times in this passage of scripture stand is mentioned. Let me say this don't ever disrupt order in disobedience. The Military understands obedience, and if they don't stand for something, they will fall for anything. Listen what the Apostle Paul says;

HAVING DONE ALL TO STAND? LISTEN! I'm standing but nothing is happening. To stand means to take up a specified position or posture, maintaining ones position.

ARE YOU STANDING IN PRAYER
                    IN STUDYING
                    IN SOWING SEED
                    IN LOVE
                    IN GIVING
                    IN FELLOWSHIP

I want this and that to happen, but ARE YOU DOING ALL? Do all and you will see victory. God has to come through for you.

Understand this, we are living in a day and time where the enemy is doing his thing BOLDFACE. Back in the day we use to say that is a boldface lie.

We can not fight the enemy in his territory. Most people who go in to spiritual warfare are not prepared for war. When people get saved they are blinded by the material and are not able to fight.

STEPS IN GOING INTO BATTLE

STEP 1: BOOTCAMP
2 TIMOTHY 2:3 THOU THEREFORE ENDURE HARDNESS, AS A GOOD SOLDIER OF JESUS CHRIST.

HARDNESS: Commander is molding you in basic training. They first take you from your surrounding environment to influence you with something different. In other words, strip you of that old identity. You can't look like you use to.

They secondly do inspection. Inspection is am I my brothers' keeper. There is always one who just wants to identify a little bit with the church, who is expecting the same manifestation. And if he doesn't get it the enemy come's in VIOLENTLY. There is pressure in kingdom training. Man up in this kingdom,

STEP2: RESEARCH AND UNDERSTAND THE ENEMIES STRATEGIES
2 TIMOTHY 2:4 NO MAN THAT WARRETH ENTANGLETH HIMSELF WITH THE AFFAIRS OF THIS LIFE; THAT HE MAY PLEASE HIM WHO HATH CHOSEN HIM TO BE A SOLDIER.

You don't have time to be worrying about your life, especially when you are going to war. Warfare is violent and destructive. God will supply all your needs. God needs you to be focused.

. 1CORINTIANS 7:35 AND THIS I SPEAK FOR YOUR OWN PROFIT; NOT THAT I MAY CAST A

SNARE UPON YOU, BUT THAT WHICH IS COMELY, AND THAT YE MAY ATTEND UPON THE LORD <u>WITHOUT DISTRACTIONS.</u>

MATTHEW 6:33 SEEK YE FIRST THE KINGDOM OF GOD AND HIS RIGHTEOUSNES AND ALL THESE THINGS SHALL BE ADDED UNTO YOU.

The enemy does not want to fight in his own camp why? He is always in your camp.

EXODUS 15:9 THE ENEMY SAID I WILL PURSUE, I WILL OVERTAKE, I WILL DIVIDE THE SPOIL; MY LUST WILL BE SATISFIED UPON THEM; I WILL DRAW MY SWORD, MY HAND SHALL DESTROY THEM.

DEUTERONOMY 23:14 FOR THE LORD THY GOD WALKETH IN THE MIDST OF THY CAMP, TO DELIVER THEE, ANDTYO GIVE UP THINE ENEMIES BEFORE THEE; THEREFORE SHALL THY CAMP BE HOLY; THAT HE SEE NO UNCLEAN THING IN THEE AND TURN AWAY FROM THEE.

If your camp (temple) be holy the enemy can't come in

JOHN 10:10 THE THIEF COMETH NOT, BUT FOR TO STEAL, AND TO KILL, AND TO DESTROY: I AM COME THAT THEY MIGHT HAVE LIFE, AND THAT THEY MIGHT HAVE IT MORE ABUNDANTLY

How does he do this?

1 JOHN 2:16 *FOR <u>ALL</u> THAT IS IN THE WORLD, THE LUST OF THE FLESH, AND THE LUST OF THE EYES, AND THE PRIDE OF LIFE, IS NOT OF THE FATHER, BUT IS OF THE WORLD*

The key word is all. It is one way they enemy attacks us all the time. How does he do it? It is right here in 1John 2:16. *This is what the enemy uses every time;*
*LUST OF THE FLESH
*LUST OF THE EYE
*THE PRIDE OF LIFE

Let's prove it;
GENESIS 3:4-6 *AND THE SERPENT SAID TO THE WOMAN, YOU SHALL NOT SURELY DIE; FOR GOD DOTH KNOWETH THAT IN THE DAY THAT YE EAT THEREOF, THEN YOUR EYES SHALL BE OPENED, AND YE SHALL BE AS GOD'S, KNOWING GOOD AND EVIL. AND WHEN THE WOMAN SAW THAT THE TREE WAS GOOD FOR FOOD, AND THAT IT WAS PLEASANT TO THE EYES, AND A TREE TO BE DESIRED TO MAKE ONE WISE, SHE TOOK OF THE FRUIT THEREOF, AND DID IT, AND GIVE IT ALSO TO HER HUSBAND WITH HER AND HE DID EAT.*

Notice the method;
- *stop having dialog with the devil (YOUR SELF)*
- *he gave Eve a hint on the attack*
- *DAY YOU EAT - LUST OF FLESH*
- *EYES SHALL BE OPEN - LUST OF EYES*
- *YOU SHALL BE AS GODS - PRIDE OF LIFE*

VERSE 6

- *WOMAN SAW IT WAS GOOD FOR FOOD… LUST OF FLESH*
- *IT WAS PLEASNT TO EYES…. LUST OF EYE*
- *TREE DESIRED TO MAKE WISE… PRIDE OF LIFE*

The enemy used this strategy from the beginning, and the war is not over. In Luke 4 we see it again
- *command stone – lust of flesh*
- *take to high place—lust of eye*
- *throw yourself down – pride of life*

The enemy will try to show you some things. Find out what is written. Jesus said what God said. Eve questioned what God said.

STEP 3: DEVELOP A WAR PLAN
Fail to plan, you plan to fail.

NUMBERS 10:9 *AND IF YOU GO TO WAR IN YOUR LAND AGAINST THE ENEMY THAT OPPRESSETH YOU, THEN YOU SHALL BLOW AN ALARM WITH THE TRUMPETS, AND YE SHALL BE REMEMBERED BEFORE THE LORD YOUR GOD; AND YE SHALL BE SAVED FROM YOUR ENEMIES.*

****SOUND AN ALARM ------- POWER OF PRAISE*

Purpose of an alarm is to keep the enemy away.

Psalms 88:9 *MINE EYES MOURNETH BY REASON OF AFFLICTION; LORD I HAVE CALLED DAILY UPON THEE, I HAVE STRETCHED OUT MY HANDS UNTO THEE.*

Part of praising is in the hands
2SAMUEL 22:35

PSALMS 144:1

2 CORINTHIANS 10:4

There has to be a shout with the lifted hands.

STEP 4: YOU HAVE TO DEPLOY

What is it to deploy? It means to spread out to form an extended front. We are soldiers on the move.
NUMBERS 2:8-10

How do we deploy? Judah means <u>PRAISE</u>. *When you go out to battle the first thing you have to send is JUDAH!!*
JUDGES 1:1

WHO ARE WE SENDING FIRST?
Verse 2 JUDAH SAID THE LORD

2 CHRONICLES 20:20-21

WHY

WE

FIGHT

TWO

Fundamental principles for victorious living;

I am ultimately victorious from the beginning, from the day I was born, before I was formed in my mother's womb, I'm already lined up for the gold mental, not the silver, nor the bronze, but the gold at the pulpit. It's already established for everyone, but people act like they only want the silver. The enemy is after everything we have, our family, our finance, our children, our job, our marriage, etc. we have to learn to contain and maintain victory over the enemy in our life.

Let's review;

MATTHEW 11:12

Notice that the violent takes by force. We defined violent as being destructive, harsh; brutal. We liken it to being raped. This is what the enemy is doing to the church. And we act like nothing is happening. He is sneaking in and taking the minds of people and we are doing nothing about it, just because we pray to the Lord. After this lesson the devil has no win. You will be fighting back.

Remember the 4 points in the first chapter;
1). BOOTCAMP
- *strips you of your identity*
- *takes you out of your environment*
- *cuts your hair*
- *changes your clothes*

In the military, I found that they call you AIRMEN! AIRMEN COME HERE…

They say this and everybody looks. It sounds hard, but it wasn't. I begin to wonder if God said CHRISTAIN, how many would look. Listen they are

trying to link you up with everybody, that at the voice one command, everybody would move. Right now, when a command goes forth, only some people respond.
Focusing on the task at hand
All needs are taken care of

2). SEEK AND UNDERSTAND THE STRATAGIES OF THE ENEMY
   - *The lust of the flesh*
   - *The lust of the eye*
   - *The pride of life*

The enemy attacks spiritually, but its manifestations are fleshly so that you can have a fleshly reaction. Remember, we don't fight in the flesh but in the spirit.

3). DEVELOP A BATTLE PLAN
   - *lift up holy hands*
   - *battle cry*

In the Book Joshua, we learn that when you lift up praise the walls will fall.

4). YOU HAVE TO DEPLOY
Going to the battlefield, remember you never fight a battle on your own grounds.

What is the real thing I'm fighting for?
Why are we to fight?
What is the purpose?

If I don't know why I'm doing a thing, I look foolish.

1CORINTHIANS 9:24-27
Uncertainty looks foolish.

We never get to the goal. We start off with a bang, but get distracted by negativity, circumstances, and trials. Why am I fighting then? Because there is a call on your life. The call is to witness the gospel. He didn't call me to preach to be rich, buy houses etc. They are only benefits of me walking in my purpose. The call is to witness the gospel. I don't need a pulpit to operate the call on my life, I just need the Word. And because there is a call on my life, I now understand why I have to fight the enemy. AS JESUS IS, SO AM I IN THIS EARTH.

1JOHN 3:8
- *The devil sinned from the beginning*
- *You win from the beginning*

The works of the devil is set up to keep you from heaven. His works are to kill, to steal, and to destroy. What? MY WITNESS. As soon as I say I love you Jesus, people are watching all the time, listening all the time, waiting on you to mess up, looking for you to do wrong. PEOPLE ARE ALSO LOOKING FOR SOMEONE WHO IS TRUE TO THIS THING.

If I'm going to stand up and be a believer, then I have to believe that God shall supply. I don't have time to make excuses. The enemy has people looking at how we treat our life, wife, children, and people. He wants to destroy other people through us. If he can destroy my witness, he is stopping the advancement of the Kingdom, by stopping other's, by saying if that's a Christian I don't want it. That is what the enemy is after. If we can be effective in our witness, we can effectively affect everything we come in contact with, but if the enemy can messed that up he has won.

So what do I do?
I destroy the works of the devil. How?

In my marriage; I love my wife as Christ loved the church.

In my children; train them up in the way they should go and they will not depart from it when they are old.
*people will judge you based on your children
*It wants to destroy my children to destroy my witness

We don't have to be deep with it. To all who say DON'T BEAT CHILDREN, they may grow up and beat you. I do all the training up to destroy the works of the devil.

In my finances; my God shall supply all my needs. But if I walk as if my needs have not been supplied by murmuring and complaining about what I don't have my witness is messed up.

What am I saying? If God is not supplying my need the scriptures is not working. Why isn't it working for you? Maybe you are not destroying the works of the devil. So how do I destroy the works of the devil?
- over my finances
Malachi 3:10 PROVE ME

To destroy the works of the devil is simply to do the Word of God. Do what the Word says do and God

has to fulfill His promise in your life. Realize this; every time you do the Word you destroy the works of the devil. If he has nothing, he can do nothing. When you do the Word your witness is so powerful. God fulfills His promise and folk will see manifestations in your life. And they will come running to the light.
DO THE WORD....

Every time the enemy wins over you it is because it is a Word failure on your part. What happens? Your witness takes a casualty of war.

There are 2 ways the enemy attacks; everything he attacks with is COVERT, nothing is OVERT.
- *Covert is under the cover*
- *Overt is openly*

1). CHEMICAL WARFARE
This is how the enemy gets us addicted to things:
- *drugs*
- *alcohol*
- *Pornography*
- *Shopping*
- *Etc*

Example; married and lusting on other women
Off drugs but still hanging around the strip, crack house

Ephesians 5:17
We win by speaking to ourselves in spiritual

Isaiah 28:1
Pride goes before the fall. When you fall to the enemie's warfare, your light begins to fade

Luke 11:21

When you are addicted, the enemy comes in and takes your stuff and divides it. God can break any addictive habit instantly. I was addicted, but I MADE A DECISION.

2). *BIOLOGICAL WARFARE*

This is a dangerous type of warfare to the church. The military uses a term called BLOOD AGENT, which causes your blood to rebel against your own self. Instead of your blood giving you life, it now gives death. You don't know it, but the enemy has been using Biological Warfare since the beginning of time.

Genesis 4:7 *Cain and Abel*

When the enemy uses Bio warfare, his purpose is to take what is joined by blood and cause you to rebel against your brother or sister.

Malachi 7:6

Understand that you and I are joined together by the blood of Jesus Christ. The enemy is trying to taint that blood so that I can rise up against you and you against me. The Bible says a house divided can't stand. Listen you want to be a good witness, stop fighting your brothers and sister in the church. Fighting about titles, we are believers. Get over your self you don't have time to be fighting. That is what the enemy wants. If he can taint the blood in the house of God nobody will come to the house of God. Stop back- biting and devouring one another. Stop rebuking one another. Put the rebuke where it belongs.... SATAN! Nobody is rebuking the devil

1Peter 5:8

The lion is big and lazy. I don't know how, but when the lion roars he puts his roar to the ground, and some how it travels from one side to the other and comes up behind its prey as if it were behind it, which causes it prey to run straight to him.

John 10:14

Jesus said my sheep know my voice. Our success is determined on how we hear from the Word of God. That roar can be and is anything that distracts you from your CALLING

TOOLS

FOR

WARFARE

THREE

1). PRAYER

Jesus often went to a solitude place to pray. He always communicated with the Father in all situations. He understood that from the beginning of time that God loved us so much that He loved us so much that He declared war on the devil Himself. He had to send His Son as a living example to defeat the works of devil and give us the tools we need to be victorious.

There is power in prayer so much that the disciples asked Jesus to teach them how to pray.

Luke 11:1 ...*Lord, teach us to pray.*

Jesus also said that men ought to always pray and faint not.

Luke 18:1

Apostle Paul exhorted Timothy to pray for all the saints.

1Timothy 2:1-3

2). WORD OF GOD

2Timothy 2:15 tells us to *STUDY TO SHOW OURSELVES APPROVE.*

The scriptures are our ammunition for battle against the enemy's attack on our lives. If we don't have no Word in us how can we combat the wiles of the devil. When Jesus was led into the wilderness to be tempting of the devil His weapon was the Word.

James 4:7 tells us to *RESIST THE DEVIL AND HE WILL FLEE FROM YOU.*

How do we resist the devil? The Word

MATTHEW 4:1-11

The passage clearly shows us that The Word works if you work. In the last chapter I said DO THE WORD.

3). WORSHIP AND PRAISE

COLOSIANS 3:16 *LET THE WORD OF CHRIST RICHLY DWELL WITHIN YOU, WITH ALL WISDOM; TEACHING AND ADMONISHING ONE ANOTHER IN PSALMS, AND HYMNS AND SPIRITUAL SONGS, SINGING WITH GRACE IN YOUR HEARTS.*

Israel worshipped and sang praises unto the Lord before they went into battle. And while they were in worship and praise the Lord set ambushes.

In Joshua 6 the children of Israel marched around the walls of Jericho 7 times and then began to shout and the walls fell.

It is uncommon to hear references to "praise and worship" as though they were identical entities, or at least combined to form one complete whole. Praise and worship are mutually cooperative activities and are frequently very similar in the way they are outwardly expressed, but they are not one and the same. Each has its own nature and purpose. Some churches are very vocal in their praise but quite withdrawn when it comes to worship. And for others, it seems relatively easy to enter into a sweetness in worship, but they have not yet learned the dynamics of praise. Balancing the two is easier once we recognize the distinctive and functions of both praise and worship.

4). Fellowship

HEBREWS10:25 NOT FORSAKING OR NEGLECTING TO ASSEMBLE TOGETHER (AS BELIEVERS), AS IS THE HABIT OF SOME PEOPLE.....

Fellowship is vital, especially when you are fighting for your life. You don't have time for foolishness your life is on the line. Understand, eagles don't hang out with chickens. The Bible says how can two walk together unless they agree. THEY CAN'T. This is why in this day and time you really got to know who you are hanging with, moreover, who you are sitting under, God is not mocked whatever you sow that you shall also reap.

So many times we go to church for all the reasons and forget that church is really a hospital for the sick and wounded, and we begin to point the finger at what this one is doing or not doing, forgetting that on that same hand the one finger that you are pointing there are three fingers pointing back at you. When God calls us to the fellowship He wants to use us to help further His Kingdom.

5). LOVE
1 CORINTIANS 13

We all know this passage of scripture. It defines love, not hate. This is how the enemy wins most of the time because we fail to love our brothers in and sisters. How can we say we love God who we can't see and don't love the very ones we see every day? We can go to church all we want, if there is bickering and strife, arguing and backbiting, undercurrents of jealousy where is the love. God is love. He didn't treat you like that, so why do it to others. The rule is this; DO UNTO OTHERS AS YOU WANT DONE UNTO YOU. Love covers a multitude of sins. Remember God loved you and you were nowhere close to being perfect and still not. So practice walking in the love today. And when you feel that you don't want to that is a great time to start.

WHO AND WHAT IS HINDERING

YOU...

FOUR

In this life there are some many appetites that hinder us from walking in the fullness of God's blessing. John calls these things "THE LUST OF THE FLESH, THE LUST OF THE EYES, AND THE PRIDE OF LIFE". (1 John 2:12-16). And if we are not mindful of these they will entrap us, clip us up, or hit us so hard and knock you slam out. UNCONSCIENCE! Of priorities, life in general, true morals and principles, and moreover God.

There are a lot of hinderances in our faith walk that will not allow us to be honest with ourselves as well as God. Admitting our shortcomings and failures, setbacks and downfalls allows us to move forward in the things of God.

In the 2 Book of Samuel 4 there was a man whose setback in life was all because of someone else. In the heat of the moment, RUSHING. Here it is

STOP RUSHING!!

What are you rushing for? What is the hurry? So many times we rush to get to nowhere that is important. And along the way someone else is hurt. Just like here in the 2 Book of Samuel. I can't imagine how the little boy must have felt at the age of 5 to have his life hindered by a RUSH, A QUICK FIX, A DRINK. Somebody reading this knows exactly what I'm talking about. And because of this your prosperity has turned to a life of poverty.

STOP RUSHING!!

Later in the same book in chapter 9 we see that King David was in search to show kindness to someone in Johnathans family. He had a son named Mephibosheth in a town called Lo Debar. Now Lo

Debar was a place of poverty, a place where drug dealers, drug users, prostitutes, alcoholics, homosexuality, lesbianism, stealing, killing, whore mongering, and much more. You name it this area claimed it. And these are those whom Jesus was sent to save. It was not the righteous who needed a doctor, but those that were sick. Just as David sent for Mephibosheth, as Jesus called Lazarus out of the grave, God is calling us to, a come out of Lo Debar.

2 Corinthians 6:17 says **COME OUT FROM AMOUNG THEM AND BE SEPARATE, SAYS THE LORD**

At this time I'm quite sure that Mephibosheth had given up all hope for his deliverance, that there was no way out, no opportunities, no nothing. He was an outcast to society, a threat to anyone who came in contact with him. Society has already ready labeled him as "CAN'T GET IT RIGHT". This has become so embedded in his mind that he believed it himself. Until the day when someone reached out and said THE LORD HAS NEED OF YOU.

SHOW SOME KINDNESS (HESED KIND OF LOVE)

Like so many of us we can't believe this has happened to us of all people. YES YOU! The war is in your mind, get out of your mind and stop thinking that it's to late, that no one cares about you, fight the good fight of faith. God is looking for you to be a soldier in His army. Listen you may have fallen but we can get back up! According to worldly standards our past life makes us unfit for services, jobs, etc. we allow the advancements and victories in others lives scare us into a fallen state, a state in which we believe is for us.

Mephibosheth , who in the right of his father Johnathan had a prior title, his feet were lame and he was unfit for service. He was 5 years old when his father and grandfather were killed. His nurse, hearing the Philistines victory was apprehensive, that in pursuit of it they would immediately send a party to Saul's house to cut off all that pertained to it, and especially aim at her master's son was next heir to be crowned. Under the apprehension of this she fled with the child in her arms to secure him in some secret place where he could not be found, and in doing this, rushing she fell with the child in her hands, bones were broken to the point that he became lame. Lame means walking or moving is easily hampered, weak, ineffectual, (unsatisfactory)

Every time we fall we become stagnated or lame. We tend to classify ourselves on a lower degree other than the degree of God. This restricts us to move freely and progress in the things of God.

God wants is to fight so that He can show us kindness. In 2 Samuel 9 we learn several things from David;

1). To be mindful of our covenant with God
2). To be mindful of our friendships
3). To be mindful of where we came from, we were not always on top of our game. Someone is less fortunate teach them.

Remember Lo Debar is a city in Gilead, a very poor, poverty strickened. Mephibosheth lived in obscurity, in darkness, a state of being unknown. When we walk in darkness people don't know us and we are well forgotten. In this frame of life we don't realize the house in which we fell from.
1 PETER 2:9
WE ARE CALLED OUT OF DARKNESS

A). Fear not
B). Bless us
   …… Found favor

Verse 8. We always feel that we are not worthy or suitable for the things that God wants to bless us with, so we begin to ask why.

C). Must be humble
   He who humbles himself will be exalted in due season. God has called us all to set at His table. Do you know that the battle you are fighting belongs to the Lord. That He has prepared a table for you before your enemies. Do you even know what table you are eating at?
1 CORINTHIANS10:21

Stop opposing God's anointing. Dead dogs you are not. Regardless of your condition, your position in life right now, no matter how much you think you have messed up, GOD CAN AND WILL BLESS YOU..

UNDERSTANDING

THE

ARMOR

OF GOD

FIVE

THE ARMOR OF GOD

THE BELT OF TRUTH: *This protects us against Satan, the father of lies.*

In the ancient world, a soldier's belt not only kept his armor in place, but it was wide enough, as a girdle, to protect his kidneys and other vital organs. Just so, the Truth protects us. Practically applied to us today you might say the Belt of Truth holds up our spiritual pants so that we're not exposed and vulnerable.

Jesus Christ called Satan the father of lies, and deception is one of the enemy's oldest tactics. We can see through Satan's lies by holding them up against truth of the Bible. The Bible helps us defeat lies. Thus the truth of God's Word shines its light of integrity into our lives and holds together all of our spiritual defenses.

THE BREASTPLATE OF RIGHTEOUSNESS: *This symbolizes the righteousness we receive by believing in Jesus Christ.*

The Breastplate of Righteousness guards our heart. A wound to the chest can be fatal. That is why ancient soldiers wore a breastplate covering their heart and lungs. Our heart is susceptible to the wickedness of this world, but our protection is the Breastplate of Righteousness, and the righteousness comes from Jesus Christ. We cannot become righteous through our own good works. When Jesus died on the cross, His righteousness was credited to all who believed in Him. Through justification, God sees us as sinless because of what His Son did on the cross for us. Accept your Christ-given righteousness. Let it cover you and protect you. Remember that it can keep your heart pure and strong for God.

SHOD YOUR FEET WITH THE GOSPEL OF PEACE: *This is symbolized by sturdy protective sandals.*

Ephesians 6:15 talks about fitting your feet with the readiness that comes from the Gospel of Peace. Terrain was rocky, requiring sturdy, protective footwear. On the battlefield or near a fort the enemy might scatter barbed spikes or sharp stones to slow an army down. In the same way Satan scatters traps for us as we are trying to spread the gospel. The Gospel of Peace is our protection, reminding us that it is by grace that souls are saved. We can sidestep Satan's obstacles when we remember John 3:16

FOR GOD SO LOVED THE WORLD THAT HE GAVE HIS ONLY BEGOTTEN SON THAT WHOSOEVER BELIEVES ON HIM SHALL NOT PERISH BUT HAVE EVERLASTING LIFE*.*

Fitting our feet with the readiness of peace is described in 1 Peter 3:15

THE SHIELD OF FAITH: *Our Shield of Faith turns aside Satan's flaming arrows.*

No defensive armor was as important as a shield. It fended off arrows, spears, and swords. Our Shield of Faith guards us against one of Satan's deadliest weapons, DOUBT. Satan shoots doubt at us when God does not act immediately or visibly. But our faith in God's trustworthiness comes from the infallible Word of God. We know our Father can be counted on. Our Shield of Faith sends Satan's arrows to the side. We keep our shield up high, and confident in the knowledge that God provides, protects and is faithful to His children. Our shield holds because of the One our faith is in Jesus Christ

THE HELMET OF SALVATION: *This is a vital protection for our minds.*

The Helmet of Salvation protects the head, where all thoughts and knowledge resides. Jesus Christ said "IF YOU HOLD TO MY TEACHING THAN YOU ARE MY DISCIPLES INDEED. AND YOU SHALL KNOW THE TRUTH AND THE TRUTH SHALL SET YOU FREE. JOHN 8:31-32

The truth of salvation through Christ does indeed set us free from vain searching, free from meaningless temptations of this world, and from condemnation of sin. Those who reject God's plan of salvation will battle Satan unprotected and suffer the fatal blow of hell.

1 Corinthians 2:16 tells us that we have the mind of Christ

2 Corinthians 10:5 explains that those who are in Christ have divine power to cast down imaginations and pull down strongholds.

The Helmet of Salvation is to protect our thoughts and minds. It is a crucial piece of armor, we cannot survive without it.

THE SWORD OF THE SPIRIT: *This represents the Bible, our weapon against Satan.*

The Sword of the Spirit is the only offensive weapon in the Armor of God in which we can strike against Satan. This weapon represents the Word of God.

HEBREWS 4:12 SAYS "THE WORD OF GOD IS ALIVE AND POWERFUL, SHARPER THAN A TWO-EDGE SWORD.

When Jesus was tempted in the desert by Satan He countered back with the truth of Scripture, setting an example for us. Satan's tactics have not changed, so the Sword of the Spirit, the Bible, is still our best defense. Commit the Word to your memory and to your heart.

PRAYER: *The Power of Prayer lets us communicate with God, the Commander of our life.*

Ephesians 6:18

Every smart soldier knows he must keep the line of communication open to their commander. God has orders for us through His Word and the prompting of the Holy Spirit. Satan hates it when we pray. He knows that prayer strengthens us and keeps us alert to his deceptions. Apostle Paul also cautions us to pray for others as well.

With the full Armor of God and the Gift of Prayer, we can be ready for whatever the enemy throws at us.
MAY GOD BLESS YOU AS YOU FAITH THE GOOD FIGHT OF FAITH.

SIX

LESSONS LEARNED

THE OPPORTUNITY TO SECURE OURSELVES AGAINST DEFEAT LIES IN OUR OWN HANDS, BUT THE OPPORTUNIY OF DEFEATING THE ENEMY IS PROVIDED BY THE ENEMY HIMSELF.

KNOW YOUR ENEMY AND KNOW YOURSELF AND YOU CAN FIGHT A HUNDRED BATTLES WITHOUT DISASTER.

ALL MEN CAN SEE THESE TACTICS WHEREBY I CONQUER, BUT WHAT NONE CAN SEE IS THE STRATEGY OUT OF WHICH VICTORY IS ENVOVLED.

HE WHO KNOWS WHEN HE CAN FIGHT AND WHEN HE CANNOT WILL BE VICTORIOUS.

YOU HAVE TO BELIEVE IN YOUSELF.

ALL WAR IS DECEPTION.

GOD BLESS

NOTES

NOTES

NOTES

NOTES

NOTES

NOTES

NOTES

NOTES

NOTES

NOTES